# I wish I could... READ!

## A story about making friends

Tiziana Bendall-Brunello

Illustrated by John Bendall-Brunello

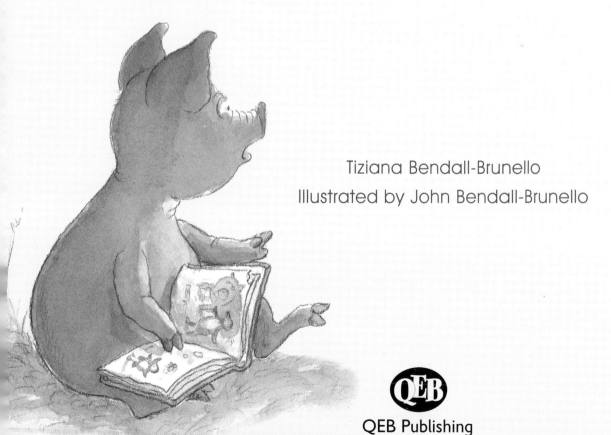

QEB
QEB Publishing

"Hey, Cow! Look what I found!" said
Little Pig. He bent down to pick up
something lying on the path.

"It's a book!" said Cow, who was lying on the cool grass nearby.

"What's a book for?"
asked Little Pig.

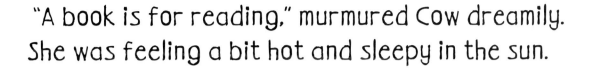

"A book is for reading," murmured Cow dreamily.
She was feeling a bit hot and sleepy in the sun.

"Oh, I wish I could read," sighed Little Pig. "Can you show me how, Cow?"
   "Mmm, all right," replied Cow. "Put it on my head!"

"Doesn't it look lovely?" said Cow.
"And see how well it keeps the sun off me!"

Cow lay down again. "Do you want to try it on?" she asked.

"Mmm," said Little Pig. "That doesn't really seem right to me!" A moment later, Cow fell fast asleep in the warm sunshine.

Little Pig quietly picked up the book and went off.

"I think I'll find another friend to help me," he thought. "Perhaps Hen will know how to read."

"Hello, Hen! Look what I found!"
said Little Pig.
   "Oh, hello!" clucked Hen. "What is it now?"

"It's a book!" said Little Pig excitedly. "Cow said that a book is for reading, but I don't know how."

"I wish I could read..." he sighed. "Do you know how, Hen?"

"Oh, yes, I think so!" said Hen.
"You just have to sit on it, like this!"

She wriggled a bit,

and then bustled a bit, and before too long she had laid an egg...

...and then another!

"But that's not reading!" exclaimed Little Pig. "I need a friend who really knows how to read."

So Little Pig turned and walked off with the book when... BOFF!

Little Pig bumped right into Goat.

The book flew up into the air...

BOFF!

"Oh, look! A book!" shouted Goat,
and he caught it with his teeth.

"What are you doing with this book?" asked Goat. "Are you learning to read, Little Pig?"

"Well, I wish I could read," replied Little Pig,
"but I can't find a friend to help me.
Could you show me how?"

"Well," said Goat, "before you learn to read you have to..." And without another word, he began to munch a corner of the book.

"Hey!" called Little Pig." I know you're hungry, but you mustn't eat my book!"

Little Pig sat down on the grass. "Oh, if only I had a friend who knew how to read..." he sighed.

"I do!" came a small voice behind Little Pig. It was the little boy.
    "I can help you," he said. "Would you like me to?"

"Oh, yes please!" said Little Pig.

And so Little Pig and his new friend went off to read the book together.

Little Pig was very happy. He had a new friend...and he was learning to READ!

And look who came peeking around the barn door to listen!

# Notes for parents and teachers

- Look at the front cover of the book together. Ask the children if they have seen a pig. Discuss what pigs eat and the kind of noise they make.

- Ask the children about their friends. What are their names? How old are they? Do they live nearby? Do the children have a best friend?

- Ask the children why they think it's important to have friends. Do they like to make new friends, for example at nursery school? Talk about what the children like doing with their friends.

- Ask the children to draw each of the animals in the book and to color in their pictures. What do these animals eat?

- Ask the children if they like to drink milk. Which foods that they eat are made from milk? Do the children like to eat eggs? Have they seen newly laid eggs?

- Ask the children about their favorite books. What kind of stories do they like to hear? Who reads the books to them, and when? Do they buy books from a bookstore or do they borrow them from a library? What other things can children do at their library?

- Ask the children to draw a picture of their favorite book. Ask them to describe how they feel when someone reads them their favorite stories.

Consultant: Cecilia A. Essau
Professor of Developmental
Psychopathology
Director of the Centre for Applied
Research and Assessment in Child and
Adolescent Wellbeing, Roehampton
University, London

Editor: Jane Walker
Designer: Fiona Hajée

Copyright © QEB Publishing, Inc. 2011

Published in the United States by
QEB Publishing, Inc.
3 Wrigley, Suite A
Irvine, CA 92618

www.qed-publishing.co.uk

ISBN 978 1 60992 067 8

Printed in China

Library of Congress Cataloging-in-Publication Data

Bendall-Brunello, Tiziana.
 I Wish I Could READ!: A story about making friends / Tiziana
Bendall-Brunello ; illustrated by John Bendall-Brunello.
   p. cm. --  (I wish I could--)
 Summary: When Little Pig finds a book he asks other farm animals
if they can teach him to read, but while each as his or her own idea
of what to do with the book, only the boy who lost it can help.
 ISBN 978-1-60992-109-5 (library bound)
[1. Books and reading--Fiction. 2. Pigs--Fiction. 3. Domestic animals-
-Fiction.]  I. Bendall-Brunello, John, ill. II. Title. III. Series.

PZ7.B431352Re 2012
[E]--dc22

2011003285